Matthew Geden

FRUIT

SurVision Books

First published in 2020 by
SurVision Books
Dublin, Ireland
Reggio di Calabria, Italy
www.survisionmagazine.com

Copyright © Matthew Geden, 2020

Design © SurVision Books, 2020

ISBN: 978-1-912963-16-4

This book is in copyright. No part of this publication may be reproduced, stored in a retrieval system, or transmitted in any form or by any means without the prior permission in writing from the publisher.

Acknowledgements

Grateful acknowledgement is made to the editors of the following, in which some of these poems, or versions of them, originally appeared:

Free Verse: "Stolen Parables"

Poetry Salzburg Review: "Sonnet I," "Sonnet II," and "Sonnet III"

Contents

Favourite Nymphs	5
The Storm	6
A Yellow Spot	7
Fish	8
Flamenco	9
Stolen Parables	10
The Back of a Lorry	15
Sonnet I	16
Sonnet II	17
Sonnet III	18
Refuge	19
Fruit	
i crescent moon	20
ii the mirror takes you	21
iii you are cold as a night bus	22
iv i will follow you through towns	23
v here in this image of green birth	24
vi sleeping in the coldness	25
vii we arrive at the faithful fruit	26
viii there's a defiance	27
ix stalk the night	28
x and if water really becomes	29
xi the simple man	30
xii enfold the heart	31
xiii she waits at the door	32
xiv the army is the colour	33
xv no-one really knows	34
xvi your love	35

Favourite Nymphs

The word *favourite* is to be interpreted
variously. I include some shrimps
and beetles. I doubt if the trout
cares. The old flies have many years
of life left in them yet. Torp's Reed
Smut Nymph, Shrimper, Eric's Beetle,
The Chomper, Gold Ribbed Hare's Ear,
The Grey Nymph, the Persuader, the Hatching
Midge Pupa, Pheasant Tail and No-Name.

The Storm

storm scientists make rain
a twist of test tubes
small clouds bump and grind
the crumbling laboratory walls

a whirl of lifetimes spin
past your eyes banknotes
flutter out of reach
tomorrow you will start over

rain and wind permitting

A Yellow Spot

The magic, a patch of sunlight
stains a wooden desk and a ghost
futility makes each line count,
nurses a way through the night.

The lion's mane spreads tentacles
pulls in her prey, slow pulse
crosses currents, a temporary
pain, dark waters at the shore.

Fish

From my luxury aquarium I see
the dark matter of the universe.

You are fattened at the table,
wonder at the ones that got away.

Flamenco

I step out of my birthday
and into confetti; a snowstorm
mutely shakes down the skies,
a furious snowglobe roused
by the Happy Dragon, the chill
of minus seven and footprints
disappear down blind *hutong*.
I grope through swirling
streets, return with *píjiǔ,*
peanuts and frozen eyelashes.
Stepping back from the cold
I open the door into Andalucia.
It is twenty eight degrees and Enrique
Morente is teaching me Flamenco,
a gift, you say, to walk two worlds at once.

Stolen Parables

i

twilight till evening leopard
the years vertical bars
changed stone love and
tearing wind suffocated
a dream this prison
may forget your symbol
precise captivity illumined
the animal destiny in
obscure machinery late
lonely purpose of wonderment
the life relates waking
and infinite to glimpse

ii

story scattered while writing
past something lost and
then a face with
parables as light force
tranquil features as magic
kaleidoscope profile perhaps
some soldiers crucified
every force was us

iii

images cause horror
threatened order could
chronicle the menace
of that scene this
sundown electing reality
stunned by animal cries
and we applauded the Gods
arrogantly aroused something
changed exaggerated talk
implacable bestial lineage
corresponded to a crimson
knife we sensed
cunning prey and fear
our revolvers killed

iv

tired of the geographies
of time contained by
a credulous reading of
enchantment in reality
survived by the dreamed
scheme in the books
that would smooth posterity
the episodes of literature
the myth and the end

v

stable shadow man
grey amidst animals
faithful and secret
inside the ditch the
black forests forgotten
awakened by the evening
a child hung and
prisoners will die
the immediate world
poorer the space and
wonderment infinite
agony is conjectured
extinguished eyes of man
fragile voice in a desk

vi

imagine a text
the handwriting of Spain
discovers a fragment
of nature hallucinatory
magic a projection
of fabulous understanding
awakens pampered delirium
a parallel cause alien
to the ancient atmosphere
a king senses the divine
condition the illusory
sword and the universe

vii

the other things happen
mechanically to know
the dictionary like
coffee but to live
justifies some pages
perhaps no one destined
to survive though
things persist in myself
books or laborious
mythologies belong to
oblivion not this page

viii

no face resembles words
only the astonishment
and outward appearance
a cure for humanity
initiated the habit
predestined the gathering
satisfaction and the flavour
ceased to become flesh
the soul disregards the
lark so many guises
in claims of existing
controlled by terror
suffering his childhood

he had concerned himself
with character excluded
his friends and found
the voice of a whirlwind
the forms are many and one

The Back of a Lorry

Fallen off the back of a lorry
nothing but the sky; an airy
emptiness that hovers above
the man-made metal, weathered
wood unsentimentally stripped
away by the years, the long
suffering blood sweat and tears
silenced by the churchyard,
a tomb marks the spot,
a stretched out wooden bed.

Sonnet I

even just to enter the surf
wrapped up in funereal black
bare blubber in the bubbles
the shock of that fierce slap
tossed around and shaped
stripped to a pale bone
thrown up on the high tide
trodden down in sand

and in silence in a car
a couple watch the waves
crash down without them
almost time to go now
the sky darkens into October
and the wind roars in their ears

Sonnet II

the art of measurement
occurs in the everyday
submission to pain
in variable light
and occasional dark
ignorant of time
one more step ahead

it's not so bad really
there is a dryness
in the throat
the muscles strain
a furious dialogue
wonders how the agony
will end the pain will die

Sonnet III

there are leaves
falling from the sky
crumpled messages
fill the many pockets
loose change gathers
a careless offering

and the metro station
fills with the air of a violin
classical elegance a concert
plays out to an unembarrassed hush
the audience flows on
ineffably towards the sea

and when the music is silent
what, after all, remains?

Refuge

What remains of summer is locked
away at night, after opening time
sun-seekers file respectfully into
a black box where a disembodied
voice in the car directs the sails
splashed in light. The beach lies
burning in the distance,
last year's tide has arrived,
rivers return to my socks,
shoes, the land, rain ravages
my throat and I seek refuge
in the conservatory of a distant country.
Years later we file out into the dark,
visas stamped in the headlights of cars.

Fruit

i

crescent moon
frowns yellow
in the basket

anonymous hands
take you home
when instructed

the sun shines
on far-off fingers
touch this memory

rapid breath now
undress beneath
the electric light

ii

the mirror takes you
through the undergrowth

tangled groves gone
wild with pithy beauty

a distant song might
call your first name

the one given to you
by the lonely earth

here in my hands
a ball of fire burns

iii

you are cold as a night bus
forests lie inside
and out
yet you will never dress
for dinner
rakish tie
dangling
live this unparalleled
life of reason
and needle
some day you will
be free of paris
the creek at dawn
so far the light
has not failed us
leads a way
i can't talk
of next spring
it isn't over
yet

iv

i will follow you through towns
narrow lanes to the sea

my night-stained hands

your song grows amongst leaves
you taste of bitterness

a worm awaits
fills your belly

the days continue
regardless of your
blackbird fate

no-one is safe
from the renaissance
the brush of colour
on cracked concrete

lie me in the bushes
cover me with rain

v

here in this image of green
birth scatters flecks of life

embeds beneath the skin
scooped out by the clock

tell me stories of liberty
driven on by the current

swept down to the shore
here in this image of green

vi

sleeping in the coldness
decay must creep further

up to the yellow kiss
the trees droop in the sun

delectable you are
don't go home

without
me

vii

we arrive at the faithful fruit
innocence at the roadside

the summer wound ribbons
around uncut hedgerows

a bewildering bond broke
down the city walls

you walk through the mirror
shimmer into the future

leave behind the false
dawn stored in a matchbox

violence is a thing endured
thrown off bridges

ideas drown in the sweet-
ness of your tongue

viii

there's a defiance
in the toughness
of your tight skin

darkness carries
its own rewards

intricate your world
tautened inks
run your veins

the rest of the world
falsifies perfection

you leave behind
an abandoned shadow
sinking like a home

ix

stalk the night
the salad days

a red cloak
your gloves

touch the air
smooth a path

for the breeze
to twist a way

to the simple
place i live

x

and if water really becomes
a dazzling ray of light
perhaps you really can climb
into the rippling heavens

make wine from your feet
survive the electrical impulse
coursing across the skies
that sweet summer sound

unearthed from the mineshaft
brought up through the rock
the heavy soil that seeps
and trickles through fingers

and you say no more
of war and poverty
try to focus on the sweet
depth of your throat

xi

the simple man
bruises easily
watches his children
consumed by mud

traitors turn to you
bury you in the crowd

he is pushed
against the wall
shakes the blood
out of his eyes

happy to be alive
and dying

happiness is in the hands
of the local assassin
a detached mouth
sings a song of plenty

when you find the bread
you no longer fear the dark

listen to my secret language
it is as old as the hand
the square root of a fallen leaf
a wave breaks upon the shore

xii

enfold the heart
in sweetness

wrap the being
in tender flesh

burst into brief
summer song

squeal all the way
down to earth

nothing is left
but stone

xiii

she waits at the door
to this latest galaxy
flicks traces of light
in waves across the cosmos
takes my hand and draws
me into her shade

this luminescence breaks
open the long sleep
becomes a daydream
in the fervent afternoon
and i watch the skies
with nothing left to say

xiv

the army is the colour
of a moonless night
wretched and useless

a manifesto dies
in every one

deserters are treated
to fine wine
tinkling of fear

shots break out
of the trees
startled wood mice

the trail is long
but the words will reach
you all the same

XV

no-one really knows
what goes on
inside you

as you lie in the sun
darkening with the leaves
on the windowsill

hands hold you
touch and prod
your longing

something like a stone
takes root

something like a heart
resists decay

xvi

your love
for the people
fills the potholes
overflows the drains
gathers in puddles
splashes in the street

my hands swallow
the dark metallic stars
the world of books
in the candlelight
a gentle music
in my veins

they will evaporate
ice in a cocktail
that sweet tang
where dreams lie
broken alcoholics
on the cusp
of evening

More poetry published by SurVision Books

Noelle Kocot. *Humanity*
(New Poetics: USA)
ISBN 978-1-9995903-0-7

Ciaran O'Driscoll. *The Speaking Trees*
(New Poetics: Ireland)
ISBN 978-1-9995903-1-4

Helen Ivory. *Maps of the Abandoned City*
(New Poetics: England)
ISBN 978-1-912963-04-1

Elin O'Hara Slavick. *Cameramouth*
(New Poetics: USA)
ISBN 978-1-9995903-4-5

John W. Sexton. *Inverted Night*
(New Poetics: Ireland)
ISBN 978-1-912963-05-8

Afric McGlinchey. *Invisible Insane*
(New Poetics: Ireland)
ISBN 978-1-9995903-3-8

Anatoly Kudryavitsky. *Stowaway*
(New Poetics: Ireland)
ISBN 978-1-9995903-2-1

Tim Murphy. *The Cacti Do Not Move*
(New Poetics: Ireland)
ISBN 978-1-912963-07-2

Tony Kitt. *The Magic Phlute*
(New Poetics: Ireland)
ISBN 978-1-912963-08-9

Clayre Benzadón. *Liminal Zenith*
(New Poetics: USA)
ISBN 978-1-912963-11-9

Thomas Townsley. *Tangent of Ardency*
(New Poetics: USA)
ISBN 978-1-912963-15-7

George Kalamaras. *That Moment of Wept*
ISBN 978-1-9995903-7-6

Anton Yakovlev. *Chronos Dines Alone*
(Winner of James Tate Poetry Prize 2018)
ISBN 978-1-912963-01-0

Bob Lucky. *Conversation Starters in a Language No One Speaks*
(Winner of James Tate Poetry Prize 2018)
ISBN 978-1-912963-00-3

Christopher Prewitt. *Paradise Hammer*
(Winner of James Tate Poetry Prize 2018)
ISBN 978-1-9995903-9-0

Mikko Harvey & Jake Bauer. *Idaho Falls*
(Winner of James Tate Poetry Prize 2018)
ISBN 978-1-912963-02-7

Tony Bailie. *Mountain Under Heaven*
(Winner of James Tate Poetry Prize 2019)
ISBN 978-1-912963-09-6

Nicholas Alexander Hayes. *Amorphous Organics*
(Winner of James Tate Poetry Prize 2019)
ISBN 978-1-912963-10-2

John Bradley. *Spontaneous Mummification*
(Winner of James Tate Poetry Prize 2019)
ISBN 978-1-912963-13-3

John Thomas Allen. *Rolling in the Third Eye*
(Winner of James Tate Poetry Prize 2019)
ISBN 978-1-912963-15-7

Gary Glauber. *The Covalence of Equanimity*
(Winner of James Tate Poetry Prize 2019)
ISBN 978-1-912963-12-6

Maria Grazia Calandrone. *Fossils*
Translated from Italian
(New Poetics: Italy)
ISBN 978-1-9995903-6-9

Sergey Biryukov. *Transformations*
Translated from Russian
(New Poetics: Russia)
ISBN 978-1-9995903-5-2

Alexander Korotko. *Irrazionalismo*
Translated from Russian
(New Poetics: Ukraine)
ISBN 978-1-912963-06-5

Anton G. Leitner. *Selected Poems 1981–2015*
Translated from German
ISBN 978-1-9995903-8-3

All our books are available to order via
http://survisionmagazine.com/books.htm

www.ingramcontent.com/pod-product-compliance
Lightning Source LLC
Chambersburg PA
CBHW061312040426
42444CB00010B/2608